Thoughts
of Love

Thoughts of Love

A collection of poems on love
Edited by Susan Polis Schutz

Blue Mountain Press ™

Boulder, Colorado

Library of Congress Number: 82-72630
ISBN; 0-88396-181-4

Manufactured in the United States of America
First Printing: September, 1982.
Second Printing: August, 1983.

The following works have previously appeared in Blue Mountain
Arts publications:

"I know I've said before," by Laine Parsons. Copyright ©
Blue Mountain Arts, Inc., 1981. "More than you know," by
Andrew Tawney. Copyright © Blue Mountain Arts, Inc., 1982.
"You are so kind," by Susan Polis Schutz. Copyright ©
Stephen Schutz and Susan Polis Schutz, 1981. "Sometimes,"
by Jamie Delere. Copyright © Blue Mountain Arts, Inc.,
1981. "When we're not together," by Andrew Tawney. Copyright
© Blue Mountain Arts, Inc., 1981.

Thanks to the Blue Mountain Arts creative staff.

ACKNOWLEDGMENTS are on page 62.

Blue Mountain Press INC.

P.O. Box 4549, Boulder, Colorado 80306

CONTENTS

7	Jan Bray	36	Edith Schaffer Lederberg
9	Laine Parsons	37	Peter A. McWilliams
11	Jacqueline Dumas	38	Michael J. Mulvena
12	Susan Polis Schutz	40	Jillien Cruse
15	Rick Norman	41	Rowland R. Hoskins, Jr.
16	Dolly Parton	42	Andrew Tawney
17	Linda DuPuy Moore	45	Jennifer Sue Oatey
18	Andrew Tawney	46	Woodrow Wilson
21	Susan Polis Schutz	47	Dorie Runyon
22	diane westlake	49	Lisa Wiggett
23	Susan Santacroce	50	Kele Daniels
24	Joni Frankel	51	Kathy Pepin
27	Daumont Valentine	52	bonnie lee harris
28	Larry Tyler	53	Hermann Hesse
29	Paul Gauguin	53	Stephen Taff
29	Claudia Adrienne Grandi	55	jonivan
30	Jamie Delere	57	Susan Polis Schutz
31	laura west	59	Rowland R. Hoskins, Jr.
33	Thomas R. Dudley	61	Janice Lamb
34	Richard W. Weber	62	Acknowledgments
35	Susan Polis Schutz		

Sometimes I wonder
if you love me
        as much as I love you . . .

I never mean to
question your love,
because I know in my heart
what I mean to you.

I guess that when I act like
        I am unsure,
all I am doing
is asking you to hold me
and tell me that
you love me.

— Jan Bray

I know I've said before
that "I love you" and have tried to
tell you how much you mean to me —
but I wonder if you really
     know how strong and sincere
my emotions are and how deeply touched
I am by your feelings.

You are such a tender and special person,
and you make me feel "special" just by
the way you talk with me, and listen with me,
and share with me the warmth of your touch
     and the desires of your heart.
I want to give so much in return —

For I do love you,
and I just wanted to let you know . . .
how nice it feels inside
     when my smile is showing
     and my heart is full
     and my thoughts are all for you.

— Laine Parsons

I promise you my love . . .
    without any limits
To accept the things
    you believe in
        and to always try
            to understand you
To be near you
    whenever you need
        my presence

To trust in your love for me
    and pray that it grows stronger every day
To watch our love grow together
    through the years

I promise to soothe your mind and body
To plan with you, dream with you
To do my best to show you
    how much I love you
For you have become my world, my heart,
    my life
The future is ours . . . always

— Jacqueline Dumas

Love is
   being happy for the other person
      when they are happy
   being sad for the person when they are sad
   being together in good times
   and being together in bad times
Love is the source of strength

Love is
   being honest with yourself at all times
   being honest with the other person at all times
   telling, listening, respecting the truth,
   and never pretending
Love is the source of reality

Love is
   an understanding that is so complete that
   you feel as if you are a part
      of the other person
   accepting the other person
      just the way they are
   and not trying to change them
      to be something else
Love is the source of unity

Love is
   the freedom to pursue your own desires
   while sharing your experiences
      with the other person
   the growth of one individual alongside of
   and together with the growth
      of another individual
Love is the source of success

Love is
   the excitement of planning things together
   the excitement of doing things together
Love is the source of the future

Love is
   the fury of the storm
   the calm in the rainbow
Love is the source of passion

Love is
   giving and taking in a daily situation
   being patient with each other's
      needs and desires
Love is the source of sharing

Love is
   knowing that the other person
   will always be with you
      regardless of what happens
   missing the other person when they are away
   but remaining near in heart at all times
Love is the source of security

Love is the
   source of life

— Susan Polis Schutz

You are a part of me . . .
        a part that
        I could
        never live without.

And I hope
        and I pray
        that I never have to.

        I love you.

                — Rick Norman

I have come to know and love you
like I've never known or loved another.
Words have not been made
that could describe the feelings
we have for each other.

I would go to any lengths
to let you know at all times that I care,
because I want you to know
that anytime you reach for me,
    you'll find me there.

— Dolly Parton

When I was young, I dreamed
of finding someone really special
who would come into my life
and love me wholly and uniquely . . .
someone who would understand my
        desires,
encourage my efforts,
and share my dreams . . .

When I grew older
I found that person:

        I love you
        for loving me
        just the way
        I dreamed it would be.

— Linda DuPuy Moore

More Than You Know . . .

I'd like to tell you
how much I love you,
and I hope you know that I do . . .
I wish that the words I speak
   so gently to you could be
heard by your heart
   with the same meanings
and the same soft feelings of love
that they carry from deep within me.

For more than you know . . .
   I love so many things about you.
More than just the way you hold me
and the warmth you give;
   I enjoy sharing life with you.
I enjoy the way we balance each other out,
how we share the good times
   and support each other through the tears,

I enjoy the knowledge that we'll make it
    through whatever life brings
with courage and with love
through the years.

More than you know . . .
    and more than I can ever say,
I feel a wonderful thankfulness
    in my heart . . . just for you.
And I want you to remember, though
    my thoughts don't always convey
    and my feelings don't always show,
I love you, and I always will . . .
    more than you know.

— Andrew Tawney

You are
  so kind
  so gentle
  so caring
You are
  so confident in yourself that
you are not afraid to show
  a strong sensitivity
  a strong vulnerability
  a strong beauty
To be so in touch
with your feelings
and emotions
is very important to me
and very important
in having a successful relationship

I want to thank you
for being such
a great person

— Susan Polis Schutz

We are given the blessing
of sharing this passage
   through time and space,
never too far apart
that our hands do not touch,
for wherever we may wander
we go with love

— diane westlake

Our life together will be worth
waiting for . . .
Time is our only obstacle and
like all things, it too will pass;
perhaps slowly, but nonetheless,
the day will come when finally
we will have the beautiful life
we've planned on.
And then we'll say
that it was surely worth
the wait.

— Susan Santacroce

I cannot give up my self for you nor do
   I want yours.
I cannot change my life's goals for you
   nor do I want you to change yours.
What I can do for you, for us, for a
   relationship consisting of you and me
Is to be a friend, companion, lover
A sharer of space and time
A comfort, support, giver.
Yet I can only do this, if you do the same,
   as a relationship is built of
   the givings of two.
To be settled and strong in this way,
   gives peace of mind and soul,
So energies can be spent on our
   purposes and not the constant
   struggle of surrendering into love.

Of your own free choice you, too,
    must enter this bond — or else there
    is no bond.
It's all the energies of the universe that
    we are confronting by calling on
    love.
It takes deep understanding and a
    strength so powerful. A commitment
    of love, purpose, goals that can be
    united and separate — overlapping.
    There cannot be anything less
    for us.

— Joni Frankel

Is it okay to feel afraid?
Because I am . . . sometimes
   afraid of taking a chance,
   afraid of losing,
   even afraid of winning sometimes.
I'm scared to love too much,
   scared to hold on too tight
   when you may want to be free;
   scared of letting go
   when I need you to hold me.
      And I need to know
      if it's okay to feel afraid,
      because sometimes I am . . .
      because I love you so much.

— Daumont Valentine

Some people see only the sun
  reflected on
    some still mountain lake . . .
You and I can feel the warmth.

Some people see the stars
  frozen against the night sky . . .
You and I see their sparkle.

Some people view the garden
  from the gate . . .
You and I walk together within.

— Larry Tyler

Everybody finds happiness
in his own way.
Happily . . .
I can think of you.

— Paul Gauguin

If I had to
spend my life without you,
I'd be forced to spend my life
        without a part of me.

You are so much of me
that loving you
is not a matter of choice . . .
        it's what I do . . .
            it's what I am.

— Claudia Adrienne Grandi

Sometimes
when I have something to tell you,
I hesitate — and wonder . . .
just how much of my feelings
I should allow to be seen,
and how you'll react to my words.

I know that I shouldn't be afraid
to tell you anything . . .
but I'm still sort of new
at being in this situation,
and I feel a little uneasy about
saying just whatever's on my mind.
But you know, don't you . . .
    of my feelings for you,
        whether they're spoken or not . . .
and my desire to open up to you
    with trust
        and with love.

— Jamie Delere

To begin a new life together
does not mean that we must forget
the lives that each of us
    leaves behind;
but rather
we should remember the differences
that brought us here;
and keep alive the memories of what
you and I are
in our pursuit of what we can
become together.

— laura west

I don't want to become
So independent
That I will think
I can make it entirely on my own
Or be so free
That I will not want
To share my life with someone
Or be in such total control
That I won't be able
To say . . .
    I want you
    I need you and
    I love you
       always.

— Thomas R. Dudley

I give to you
My heart and soul
I give to you
Life within my hand
And all happiness that I can
I give to you
Part of me
And all for what I stand
I give to you
The moment shared
When two people touch
    hand-in-hand
I give to you
The sunset
And the fallen night
With its stars so bright
I give to you
The life we can share
And all the love that I can.

— Richard W. Weber

Time passes by and
  Our love is stronger than ever
  Our love is more tender than ever
  Our love is more honest than ever
  Our love is more overwhelming
    than ever
  Our love is wilder than ever
  Our love is more exciting than ever
  Our love is more confident than ever
  Our love is more playful than ever
  Our love is more meaningful
        than ever
Time passes by and
  Our love is more lasting than ever

— Susan Polis Schutz

Love is . . .
   forgiving even though it's hard
        to forget;
   holding hands and never wanting
        to let go;
   hoping that tomorrow will be as
        wonderful as today;
   sharing secrets
        and whispers
            and star-spangled nights.
And most importantly,
Love is . . .
   knowing that you'll never
        be lonely
            again.

— Edith Schaffer Lederberg

You are a wonderful,
    worthy and loveable person.
Appreciate that
about yourself.
No one has ever been,
or ever will be,
quite like you.
You are an individual,
    an original,
and all those things that make you
uniquely you
are deserving of love
        and praise.

— Peter A. McWilliams

Sunrise was a time I never knew
   till I met you.
Mornings weren't my style,
   too bright,
   too cheerful,
      just didn't match my mood.
Nighttime seemed to always offer me
   a solace,
   a peace,
   perhaps it was only the dimming of vision
      or the cool of the darkness,
   but the less my senses had to deal with
      the better,
      the easier,
   till I met you . . .

Through the dark,
And through the steadiness,
Through the imagined peace,
    you rose like a gentle dawn,
    awakening my emotions,
    stretching my imagination,
    applying your subtle pastels
            to my desires,
    warming a coldness within my heart.
Sunrise was a time I never knew,
Morning songs were for the birds
    or dedicated joggers —
            not for me.
Till I met you.

— Michael J. Mulvena

I needed something to believe in.
You touched me with your eyes,
        and I believed.
I needed someone to believe in.
You shared yourself, your dreams,
        and I believed.
But what I really needed
was to believe in myself.
You took me within yourself
and helped me,
with the love we both shared.
And because of you
I am living
touching
believing
in something,
    in someone,
        in myself . . .
because of you.

— Jillien Cruse

I have loved you so much this day, and yet, as tomorrow dawns, my love for you is somehow growing — brighter, stronger, deeper, and somehow more warm and beautiful than before. Still, the new day will come and enact the same miracle over again. I believe our love knows no limits.

— Rowland R. Hoskins, Jr.

When we're not together . . .

    my thoughts drift alongside
        memories of you;
    things we've done
    the way you smile so brightly
    that helps me forget my worries
    and celebrates our wonders

When we're not together . . .

    my moods come into play more often
    and make me yearn for the strength
    I feel with you . . .
    the security I find in your eyes

When we're not together . . .

    I sometimes feel so very alone,
    for myself and for you . . .
    imagining you being without
    my loving feelings
    as I am without yours

When we're not together . . .

my best wishes still go with you always,
wishing to share in your excitements
wanting to comfort your hurts
needing to be reassured that
you're keeping warm and well

When we're not together . . . I seem to

spend my time
wishing that we were

— Andrew Tawney

Do you know
How comfortable you are

How easy it is
To slip into being with you

The depth of the feelings
I have for you

How easy it is to love you
And how hard it is to be apart . . .

— Jennifer Sue Oatey

I am,
in every thought
of my heart,
        yours.

— Woodrow Wilson

I will love you
not just for today
or a year from now
but within the heart of my feelings
where time can draw no boundaries.
I will love you
not just as a memory of
            a moment shared
but in every glimpse of beauty
that stirs my senses and captures
my pleasure to live.
When I walk alone
you will be the sun at my back
and the smile on my lips.
In my dreams
you will appear as the visions
I've yet to see.
Whether real or imagined
each part of my life is measured
with you at the center of love.

— Dorie Runyon

The time I have with you
Is very special.
To reach out to you
And know you'll be there —
That means all the world to me.
My heart is with you
    wherever you go,
My love is yours no matter what.

When you smile at me,
I know it's from your heart.
I know you'll do for me
What no one else would do.
And if I don't tell you
I love you
As often as I should . . .
It's because I hope that,
Deep down inside,
You know I do.

— Lisa Wiggett

Let it never be the case
that we grow
too weary, impatient
        or fearful
to sit and talk
to one another
about our love.
Let us always remember
that just sitting
and talking
to one another
is how we discovered
our love
in the first place.

— Kele Daniels

There will never exist
between two people
a bond of closeness
or commitment
that is comparable
to the strength
of the ties that bind
you and I.

The years may pass
between us
and time spent apart
may change us.

Still the promises made
the lessons learned
the bridges built
and the determination
buried deep within us
will serve only to strengthen
those ever present ties
that bind
you and I.

— Kathy Pepin

Wish we could get away
Just for a day or two
Alone,
The two of us
With nothing to do
But walk and talk,
Laugh and learn
About ourselves
And each other.

— bonnie lee harris

If I know
what love is,
it is
because
    of you.

— Hermann Hesse

Loving you is as natural
as loving sunsets,
rainbows and April showers
for they are all
simply beautiful.

— Stephen Taff

I am here
to love you . . .
to love you and to want you.
To need you, to feel you,
to touch you, to be with you.
I love you in the morning,
the middle of the day,
in the hours we are together,
and the hours you are away.
I love the old and the new,
the sunlight and the shade,
the warmth and the cool,
the smiles and the tears
for it is only because of you
that any of these things exist for me . . .
I love you because I was searching
for the true meanings of love
that I did not know
until I found them in you.

You are my love.

— jonivan

Let me be the person
that you walk with in the mountains
Let me be the person
that you pick flowers with
Let me be the person
that you tell all your inner feelings to
Let me be the person
that you talk to in confidence
Let me be the person
that you turn to in sadness
Let me be the person
that you smile with in happiness
Let me be the person
that you
love

— Susan Polis Schutz

Today . . . I have thought about you so much.
I have missed you and cherished you.
I have dreamed countless dreams of
        you and I together,
reaching for clouds and searching for stars
so that we may see and climb even higher.
I have encountered a hundred little things
that I wanted to share with you,
but you were not there,
and it made me appreciate you
and our times together even more.
Yet still, I will save all of these things
in my mind and in my heart, so that I may
share all that I am with you
in the opportunities I receive.

But for today, it is enough
to say I have lived, and that . . .
        I have fallen more in love with you.

— Rowland R. Hoskins, Jr.

I think our love
         was meant to be . . .
The special sharing we know
couldn't be as it is today
if we had not met
exactly when we did.

If our lives hadn't touched
when they did,
I might have lived today
loving one less person.
But not just any person . . .
a very beautiful one . . .

Thank you for being you,
and for helping me
to understand
some of the joys to be found
                  in life.

                    — Janice Lamb

ACKNOWLEDGMENTS

We gratefully acknowledge the permission granted by the following authors, publishers and authors' representatives to reprint poems and excerpts from their publications.

Jan Bray for "Sometimes I wonder," by Jan Bray. Copyright © Jan Bray, 1982. All rights reserved. Reprinted by permission.

Jacqueline Dumas for "I promise you my love . . ," by Jacqueline Dumas. Copyright © Jacqueline Dumas, 1982. All rights reserved. Reprinted by permission.

Rick Norman for "You are a part of me . . ," by Rick Norman. Copyright © Rick Norman, 1982. All rights reserved. Reprinted by permission.

Velvet Apple Music for "I have come to know and love you," by Dolly Parton. From the song "HOW DOES IT FEEL TO KNOW." © Copyright assigned to Velvet Apple Music, 1980. All rights reserved. Used by permission.

Linda DuPuy Moore for "When I was young," by Linda DuPuy Moore. Copyright © Linda DuPuy Moore, 1981. All rights reserved. Reprinted by permission.

Diane Westlake for "we are given the blessing," by Diane Westlake. Copyright © Diane Westlake, 1981. All rights reserved. Reprinted by permission.

Susan Santacroce for "Our life together," by Susan Santacroce. Copyright © Susan Santacroce, 1982. All rights reserved. Reprinted by permission.

Joni Frankel for "I cannot give up my self," by Joni Frankel. Copyright © Joni Frankel, 1982. All rights reserved. Reprinted by permission.

Daumont Valentine for "Is it okay to feel afraid," by Daumont Valentine. Copyright © Daumont Valentine, 1981. All rights reserved. Reprinted by permission.

Larry Tyler for "Some people see only the sun," by Larry Tyler. Copyright © Larry Tyler, 1982. All rights reserved. Reprinted by permission.

Claudia Adrienne Grandi for "If I had to," by Claudia Adrienne Grandi. Copyright © Claudia Adrienne Grandi, 1982. All rights reserved. Reprinted by permission.

Laura West for "To begin a new life together," by Laura West. Copyright © Laura West, 1982. All rights reserved. Reprinted by permission.

Thomas R. Dudley for "I don't want to become," by Thomas R. Dudley. Copyright © Thomas R. Dudley, 1982. All rights reserved. Reprinted by permission.

Richard W. Weber for "I give to you," by Richard W. Weber. Copyright © Richard W. Weber, 1982. All rights reserved. Reprinted by permission.

Edith Schaffer Lederberg for "Love is . . ," by Edith Schaffer Lederberg. Copyright © Edith Schaffer Lederberg, 1982. All rights reserved. Reprinted by permission.

Peter A. McWilliams for "You are a wonderful," by Peter A. McWilliams. Copyright © Peter A. McWilliams, 1981. All rights reserved. Reprinted by permission.

Michael J. Mulvena for "Sunrise was a time," by Michael J. Mulvena. Copyright © Michael J. Mulvena, 1982. All rights reserved. Reprinted by permission.

Jillien Cruse for "I needed something to believe in," by Jillien Cruse. Copyright © Jillien Cruse, 1982. All rights reserved. Reprinted by permission.

Rowland R. Hoskins, Jr. for "I have loved you so much this day" and for "Today . . . I have thought about you so much." Copyright © Rowland R. Hoskins, Jr., 1982. All rights reserved. Reprinted by permission.

Jennifer Sue Oatey for "Do you know," by Jennifer Sue Oatey. Copyright © Jennifer Sue Oatey, 1982. All rights reserved. Reprinted by permission.

Princeton University Press for "I am, in every thought," by Woodrow Wilson. Copyright © Princeton University Press, 1980. All rights reserved. Reprinted by permission.

A careful effort has been made to trace the ownership of poems used in this anthology in order to obtain permission to reprint copyrighted material and to give proper credit to the copyright owners.

If any error or omission has occurred, it is completely inadvertent, and we would like to make corrections in future editions provided that written notification is made to the publisher: BLUE MOUNTAIN PRESS, INC., P.O. Box 4549, Boulder, Colorado 80306.